ESSENTIAL COOK'S HINTS & TIPS

ESSENTIAL COOK'S HINTS & TIPS

Bridget Jones

LORENZ BOOKS

This edition published by Lorenz Books
an imprint of Anness Publishing Limited
Hermes House, 88-89 Blackfriars Road, London SE1 8HA

Distributed in Canada by Raincoast Books
8680 Cambie Street, Vancouver, British Columbia V6P 6M9

ISBN 0-7548-0343-0

A CIP catalogue record for this book is available from the British Library

Publisher: Joanna Lorenz
Editorial Manager: Helen Sudell
Copy Editor: Jenni Fleetwood
Designer: Bet Ayer
Jacket Design: Wilson Harvey Marketing and Design
Photographs: Karl Adamson, Edward Allwright, Steve Baxter, James Duncan, Michelle Garrett,
Nelson Hargreaves, Amanda Heywood, David Jordan, Don Last, Patrick McLeavey, Polly Wreford
Home Economists: Catherine Atkinson, Jaqueline Clark, Carole Clements, Roz Denny, Nicola Diggins, Stephanie Donaldson,
Matthew Drennan, Tessa Evelegh, Joanna Farrow, Rafi Fernandez, Christine France, Shirley Gill, Rosamund Grant,
Carole Handslip, Deh ta-Hsuiung, Sohelia Kimberley, Elizabeth Lambert Ortiz, Patricia Lousada, Gilly Love, Norma Macmillan,
Sue Maggs, Annie Nichols, Jenny Stacey, Liz Trigg, Pamela Westland, Steve Wheeler, Elizabeth Wolf-Cohen

Also published as *A Cook's Hints and Tips Book*

Printed and bound in Singapore

© Anness Publishing Limited 1998, 1999

1 3 5 7 9 10 8 6 4 2

*For all recipes, quantities are given in both metric and imperial measures
and, where appropriate, measures are also given in standard cups and spoons.
Follow one set, but not a mixture, because they are not interchangeable.*

CONTENTS

INTRODUCTION

Every cook has a collection of valued recipes, often on tatty scraps of paper and usually supplemented by a selection of books on a wide variety of food subjects. Occasionally, the spark of inspiration needed when dreaming up a family supper or planning a dinner-party menu is not a detailed recipe but an idea for preparing ingredients, combining flavours or using a simple cooking technique.

In the following pages there are hints for all sorts of cooks and every occasion. Suggestions range from practical reminders on subjects like storing food safely to useful tips for garnishing dinner party dishes. Cooking times and basic techniques are supplemented by quick ways of using simple ingredients, such as fruit, and reminders on how to make the most of classics, like sauces.

This is a little book of culinary snippets – ideas for making life a lot easier in the kitchen. Easy to dip into, there is a wealth of advice plus detailed step-by-step photographs of the basic cookery techniques and skills.

Weighing and Measuring

While many wonderful meals result from impromptu "throw-it-all-in" cooking sessions, an equal number of culinary disasters are the disappointing outcome of simple mistakes or misunderstandings when weighing and measuring ingredients.

USEFUL CONVERSIONS

It is important to follow only one set of measures, metric or imperial, when using a recipe because they are not necessarily interchangeable.

LIQUID/CAPACITY MEASURES

ml = millilitre(s)   fl oz = fluid ounce(s)

Metric	Imperial
150ml	¼ pint
250ml	8fl oz
300ml	½ pint
350ml	12fl oz
475ml	16fl oz
600ml	1 pint
750ml	1¼ pints
900ml	1½ pints
1 litre (1000ml)	1¾ pints
1.2 litres	2 pints

Pint measures listed here are British pints, which equal 600ml (2½ cups). An American pint equals 475ml (16fl oz).

WEIGHTS

g = gram(s) oz = ounce(s)

Metric	Imperial
10g	¼ oz
15g	½ oz
20g	¾ oz
25g	1oz
40g	1½ oz
50g	2oz
65g	2½ oz
75g	3oz
90g	3½ oz
115g	4oz
225g	8oz
275g	10oz
350g	12oz
450g	1lb
900g	2lb
1kg	2¼ lb

SPOON MEASURES

tsp = teaspoon(s)   tbsp = tablespoon(s)

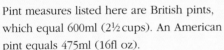

1.5ml	¼ tsp
2.5ml	½ tsp
5ml	1 tsp
15ml	1 tbsp

3 tsp = 1 tbsp (British and American) The Australian tablespoon measure holds 20ml or 4 x 5ml (1 tsp) measures.

When pouring liquid into a measuring spoon, do not hold the spoon over the bowl or pan in case you accidentally pour some into the mixture.

OVEN TEMPERATURES

Oven temperatures are usually given for standard ovens. Forced convection ovens cook significantly faster, allowing the temperature to be reduced by 20°C compared to that used in a traditional oven, or for the cooking time to be shortened by about 10 minutes, depending on the food. Check the manufacturer's instructions and recommended cooking temperatures and times for your appliance. If you are cooking two or more hot dishes, make sure that they can be staggered or have the same cooking temperatures.

Centigrade	Fahrenheit	Gas Mark
110°C	225°F	Gas ¼
120°C	250°F	Gas ½
140°C	275°F	Gas 1
150°C	300°F	Gas 2
160°C	325°F	Gas 3
180°C	350°F	Gas 4
190°C	375°F	Gas 5
200°C	400°F	Gas 6
220°C	425°F	Gas 7
230°C	450°F	Gas 8
240°C	475°F	Gas 9

CUP MEASURES

Capacities

¼ cup = 50ml/2fl oz
⅓ cup = 75ml/2½fl oz
½ cup = 120 ml/4fl oz
⅔ cup = 150ml/5fl oz
¾ cup = 175ml/6fl oz
1 cup = 250ml/8fl oz

CUP WEIGHT EQUIVALENTS

When using cups to measure dry ingredients, it is important to remember that cups measure volume, so the weight varies according to how heavy the particular item is. The following are a few examples.

Ingredient	1 cup weighs
Breadcrumbs, fresh	50g/2oz
Breadcrumbs, dry	115g/4oz
Butter	225g/8oz
Cheese, grated	115g/4oz
Cornflour	115g/4oz
Cornmeal	115g/4oz
Couscous	175g/6oz
Currants	175g/6oz
Flour	115g/4oz
Oats, rolled	90g/3½oz
Raisins	150g/5oz
Rice, long-grain	200g/7oz
Sugar, brown (packed)	225g/8oz
Sugar, white	225g/8oz

USING A MEASURING JUG

Put the jug on a level surface, pour in the liquid, then bend down so that the jug is at eye level and check the volume of liquid against the markings on the side of the jug.

USING CUPS AND SPOONS

All cup and spoon measures should be level. Scoop up ingredients, then use the blunt edge of a knife to level the top. If a recipe calls for a "packed" cup or spoon of something, pack in the ingredient with the blade of the knife. When using a spoon or cup to measure liquids, carefully fill the spoon or cup to the brim.

THE BEST WAY TO MEASURE

Cooks with years of experience may not need to measure ingredients, but if you are a beginner it is best to follow instructions carefully.

Weigh dry ingredients (sugar, flour) first as they will leave the pan on the scales clean. If you have to weigh sticky items first, line the pan with a piece of clear plastic wrap or greaseproof paper to save washing the scale pan up.

Never measure raw ingredients that are about to be cooked (fish, seafood, chicken, meat) followed by any items which are to be served raw (such as butter to make a herb butter topping for grilled meat) without thoroughly washing and drying the pan or container.

HONEY, SYRUP AND TREACLE

If you have to spoon a sticky ingredient out of the container, heat a metal spoon in boiling water or over a gas flame first and the honey or syrup will slide off it easily. When using a plastic measuring spoon, use a

round-bladed knife to level the top of the full spoon and to scrape off excess from around the side, then scrape out all the measured syrup.

If you have scales on which you can stand a mixing bowl, put it in position, zero the scales and then pour the ingredient directly into the bowl.

BUTTER AND OTHER FATS

When a recipe calls for a quantity of melted butter, remember that the butter will occupy the same volume and weigh the same whether it is melted or solid, so measure or weigh it first, then melt it.

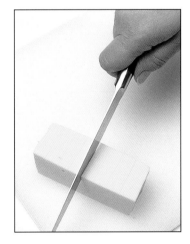

You may have noticed markings on butter packs – if you are using a new pack, then cut off the required amount level with the marking on the packet. If there are no markings, check the weight of the pack and divide it into usable portions, then cut off the required amount with a knife and place it on the scales.

PREPARED AND COOKED WEIGHTS

It is sometimes useful to know how much items will weigh once they have been cooked or prepared.

Apples (Cooking)

450g/1lb whole apples yield about 350g/12oz/ 3½ cups slices.

450g/1lb prepared, cooked apples yield about 475ml/16fl oz/2 cups unsweetened purée.

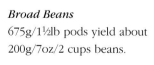

Breadcrumbs

175g/6oz/3 cups fresh white bread yields about 125g/4¼ oz/1¾ cups fine dry white crumbs.

Broad Beans

675g/1½lb pods yield about 200g/7oz/2 cups beans.

Chestnuts

450g/1lb whole yield about 350g/12oz peeled cooked chestnuts.

Chick Peas

225g/8oz/1¼ cups dried peas weigh about 425g/ 15oz/3 cups when cooked (equivalent to the drained contents of 2 x 425g/15oz cans).

Crab

1 average crab yields about 350g/12oz meat.

Lemon

1 fresh lemon yields about 45–60ml/3–4 tbsp juice.

Grapefruit
1 grapefruit yields about
90–150ml/8–10 tbsp/
1 cup juice.

Red Kidney Beans
225g/8oz/1¼ cups dried
beans weigh about
450g/1lb/3 cups when
cooked (equivalent to the
drained contents of
2 x 425g/15oz cans).

Rice
175g/6oz/¾ cup
raw rice yields
450g/1lb/1¾ cups
cooked rice.

Parmesan Cheese
25g/1oz very finely
chopped or finely
grated fresh Parmesan
equals about 30ml/2
tbsp.

Peas
450g/1lb
pods yield
about
175g/6oz/1½
cups peas.

Spinach
450g/1lb raw
spinach yields about
225g/8oz/2 cups cooked.

SERVING PORTIONS

Carrots
Allow 115–175g/
4–6oz per portion.
When serving raw
carrot sticks with a
dip, allow 65g/2½oz
per portion.

Duck
A roast 2.75kg/6lb
duck will provide
4 portions if jointed;
it will only provide
3 portions of easily
carved meat; allow
2 ducks to provide
6 portions.

**Leaf Vegetables e.g.
cabbage**
Allow 115–175g/
4–6oz cabbage (raw)
per portion. Use
slightly more
spinach as it shrinks
considerably.

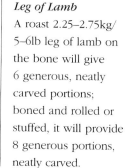

Fish
Fish the size of trout
and mackerel will
provide one portion
each; fillets of fish,
such as plaice, are
served singly or in
pairs (when rolled);
you should allow
115–175g/4–6oz
white or smoked fish
fillet per portion.

Chicken
A roast 1.25–1.5kg/
3–3½ lb chicken will
provide 4 portions of
carved meat, not all
uniformly sized;
boned and stuffed,
the same bird will
provide 6 neat,
generous portions.

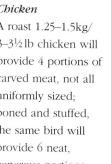

Leg of Lamb
A roast 2.25–2.75kg/
5–6lb leg of lamb on
the bone will give
6 generous, neatly
carved portions;
boned and rolled or
stuffed, it will provide
8 generous portions,
neatly carved.

Peas
450g/1lb fresh peas from pods will serve 2.
Allow 115g/4oz of shelled peas per portion.

Roast Beef
Allow 75–115g/3–4oz carved meat per portion; a
1kg/2¼lb joint of boned meat will give 4 portions.

Potatoes
Allow 225g/8oz of new potatoes per portion. Allow 1
medium old potato per portion or half of a very large
potato, when boiling; when roasting, allow 1–1½
medium old potatoes or ¾ very large old potato.

Pasta
Allow 75–90g/3–3½oz per portion when cooking as an
accompaniment. Allow 90–175g/3½–6oz when using as
the main ingredient.

Stewed Cubed Meat
Stewed with vegetables (a selection of onions, carrots,
celery, mushrooms), 450g/1lb provides 4 healthy
servings. In a simple casserole without a substantial
selection of vegetables allow 675g/1½lb for 4 servings.

Rice
Allow 50g/2oz of raw rice per portion when cooking
as an accompaniment. Allow 75–115g/3–4oz when
using as the main ingredient in a dish such as risotto.

REFRIGERATOR AND FREEZER
REMINDERS

*R*efrigerators and freezers make life far easier for busy cooks,
making for fewer shopping trips and safer food storage. Both must be kept
scrupulously clean and they must run efficiently to ensure they are safe.

TEMPERATURE CHECK

✳ A freezer alarm provides an audible warning if the inside becomes too warm – this is useful if the door of an upright freezer has not been shut properly.

✳ Open the door only briefly to prevent warm air outside entering and cold air escaping; avoid standing in front of the open fridge, wondering what on earth to cook for dinner!

✳ Internal temperatures should be no higher than: Fridge – 5°C/41°F. Freezer – 18°C/0°F.

Use the fast-freeze setting on your freezer for successful ice creams and sorbets.

FAST-FREEZE SETTING

This reduces the temperature to a minimum and compensates when a batch of fresh food is frozen.

✳ The quicker the food is frozen, the better the result, so always use this setting when freezing a significant quantity of food.

✳ Turn on the fast-freeze setting about 30–60 minutes in advance (check manufacturer's instructions); do this before making ice creams and sorbets to reduce the proportion of ice crystals.

APPLIANCE HYGIENE TIPS

✳ It is important to clean the fridge regularly and defrost it according to the manufacturer's instructions, if necessary. Any spills must be wiped up immediately and the surrounding area cleaned.

✳ Empty the fridge completely when cleaning, remove all racks and door-hung containers.

✳ Wipe the interior with hand-hot water to which 5ml/1 tsp bicarbonate of soda has been added for every 600ml/1 pint/2½ cups. Alternatively, use a weak solution of bleach or sterilizing fluid (the type used for babies' bottles). Do not use strong-smelling or abrasive cleaning agents.

✳ Use a blunt plastic scraper to remove any build-up of ice regularly and to scrape off the excess ice when defrosting the freezer.

✳ Do not use a knife, metal scraper or sharp object which could damage the lining of the freezer or any pipework located in the interior.

✳ Do not use an artificial heat source to defrost the freezer – this can cause severe damage to the appliance.

✳ Stand a bowl of hot water in the freezer to help thaw the ice quickly.

✳ Wipe out the inside of the freezer as when cleaning the fridge.

TIPS FOR REMOVING UNPLEASANT ODOURS

If you have unpleasant odours in the fridge or freezer, first check the contents and make sure it is not coming from any food items. Then clean the appliance thoroughly. If there are lingering odours, place an unwrapped cut lemon in the fridge or freezer for a few days.

WRAP AND STACK

A selection of wraps and storage containers.

IN THE FREEZER

✳ Use airtight freezer containers or heavy gauge polythene bags.

✳ Exclude as much air as possible from bags and close them with wire ties.

✳ Label food with the type, date and any notes such as whether sugar is added to apple purée or if stock needs diluting with water.

IN THE REFRIGERATOR

✳ All food should be wrapped or covered to prevent odours from being transferred and to stop the flavour of delicate foods (such as eggs, butter or milk) being tainted by strong foods (like fish, smoked foods or garlic sausage).

✳ Food which is bought in sealed packs should be stored in them; once opened, any unused food should be re-wrapped.

✳ Raw foods which are eaten cooked (such as fish, poultry, meat) must be placed in containers deep enough to hold juices, and covered.

CROSS-CONTAMINATION

✳ Raw items that are cooked before they are eaten must not touch cooked foods. Bacteria from items such as fish, chicken and meat can contaminate cheese, cooked foods and salads, causing cross-contamination and possibly resulting in food poisoning.

TOP-TO-BOTTOM ORDER

✳ Warm air rises, so the top shelves are not as cool as the bottom shelves, which are usually coldest, particularly in larder fridges (without ice boxes).

✳ In some fridges, the area just beneath the ice box is coldest.

✳ Place highly perishable items such as raw fish, poultry, meat and meat products on the coldest shelf.

✳ Store cooked fish, poultry and meat, cheese, butter and dairy desserts on the next shelf.

✳ Keep eggs in their cartons, sealed containers of fruit juice and vegetables on the next shelf. If there is a vegetable drawer, wrap vegetables and salad produce and place them in it.

✳ Place milk, commercial mayonnaise and similar opened products, such as jams and preserves, on the door shelves.

✳ Do not store highly perishable items on the door shelves as this area is exposed to warm air when the door opens.

The door compartment in the fridge is ideal for storing bottles.

TIME-SAVING FREEZER STANDBYS

INSTANT THICKENER

Make beurre manié: cream together 225g/8oz each of butter (1 cup) and plain flour (2 cups). This will thicken 3.5–4.8 litres/6–8 pints/15–20 cups of liquid. Shape it into a thick oblong and chill. Grate the mixture and open-freeze it on a tray lined with clear film. When frozen hard, store in a bag. Sprinkle small amounts into simmering soups, sauces or casseroles, whisking or stirring vigorously, and simmer until thickened.

TWISTS OF RIND

Grate citrus rind on to a piece of clear film, tip it together and twist the film. Freeze in a sealed container. For shreds, pare off strips and cut them into fine shreds. Once you have a bag "on the go" in the freezer, add twists of rind whenever you have a surplus. Each twist should hold the rind of one fruit.

QUICK CRUMBLE

Make and freeze a large batch of basic crumble mix, using a half quantity of butter or margarine to plain flour. Rub the fat into the flour, then freeze the breadcrumb-like mixture. Use frozen, to top fruit, stirring in a little brown sugar and ground mixed spice, or for savoury mixtures (such as fish, ham or vegetables in cheese sauce, or meat sauce), adding seasoning, grated cheese and chopped spring onions.

VEGETABLE STOCK

Makes about 2 litres/3½ large pints/8cups

INGREDIENTS
2 large onions, coarsely chopped
2 leeks, sliced
2 large carrots, sliced
6 celery stalks, coarsely chopped
a large strip of lemon zest
a handful of parsley sprigs with stalks
a few fresh thyme sprigs
2 bay leaves
2.5 litres/4 pints/9 cups water

Put the vegetables, herbs and water in a saucepan and bring to the boil. Reduce the heat and simmer, uncovered, for 45 minutes. Strain and leave it to cool. Cover and refrigerate for up to 5 days.

STRAWBERRY ICE

Purée 500g/1¼lb/3 cups strawberries with 90g/3½ oz/ scant ½ cup caster sugar and 120ml/4fl oz/½ cup orange juice. Be sure the sugar has dissolved completely. Taste and add more sugar if required. The mixture should be slightly too sweet as it will taste less so when frozen. Chill well then transfer to an ice cream machine and freeze until firm. Alternatively, freeze in a container, whisking two or three times when part frozen.

PESTO

Pesto will keep for months in the fridge when stored in jars cleaned with a sterilizing solution first. It is best to store the pesto in small jars so that the contents can be used up in one go.

Makes about 600ml/1 pint/2¹/₂ cups

INGREDIENTS
50g/2oz/2 cups basil leaves and sprig tops
6 garlic cloves
115g/4oz/1¹/₃ cups pine nuts
115g/4oz/1¹/₃ cups freshly grated Parmesan cheese
475ml/16fl oz/2 cups olive oil
salt and ground black pepper

Strip any tough stalks from the basil. Combine the basil with the garlic and pine nuts in a food processor or blender until finely chopped and well mixed.

Add the Parmesan cheese and about a third of the oil. Process the mixture for a few seconds, then slowly pour in the remaining oil, with the motor running, to make a smooth paste. Add seasoning to taste. Pour the paste into sterilized jars, cover tightly and leave to settle for 24 hours. Check that the surface of the paste is covered with a layer of oil; if it is not pour a little olive oil over the top. Store in the fridge.

TIPS FOR USING PESTO
* Pesto makes a tasty filling for baked potatoes.
* Mixed with soured cream or soft cheese, pesto makes a terrific dip, particularly with vegetables such as celery, carrots or fennel sticks.
* Fill grilled large mushrooms with a spoonful of pesto and serve on hot, buttered toast.
* Enliven egg mayonnaise by swirling a little pesto into the mayonnaise before coating the eggs.

Pasta with pesto.

SALAD DRESSINGS

These are a practical freezer standby. A jar of good-quality bought mayonnaise can be turned into toppings for baked potatoes or pasta, tasty dips, or a variety of sauces for fried and grilled food.

TOMATO MAYONNAISE

Flavour the mayonnaise with a little tomato purée, a squeeze of lemon juice and chopped capers. Good with prawns (cold) or seafood fritters.

GARLIC MAYONNAISE

Add a crushed garlic clove and serve the mayonnaise as a dip or as a topping for toasted French bread to serve with soup. Season this with cayenne pepper to make a hot *rouille* to serve with lobster *bisque* or other fish soups.

ORANGE MAYONNAISE

Add grated orange rind and chopped spring onion to make a tangy condiment for grilled pork sausages or pork chops.

VINAIGRETTE DRESSING

A good vinaigrette can do more than dress salad. It can also be used to baste meat, poultry, seafood or vegetables during cooking; and it can be used as a flavouring and tenderizing marinade. The basic mixture of oil, vinegar and seasoning lends itself to many variations. The basic vinaigrette dressing will keep in the refrigerator, in a tightly closed container, for several weeks. Add flavourings, particularly fresh herbs, just before using.

Makes about 175ml/6 fl oz/³/₄ cup

INGREDIENTS
3 tbsps wine vinegar
salt and pepper
150ml/¹/₄ pint/²/₃ cup vegetable oil

Put the vinegar, salt and pepper in a bowl and whisk to dissolve the salt. Gradually add the oil, stirring with the whisk. Taste and adjust seasoning.

TIPS FOR VINAIGRETTE
✴ Try using lemon juice instead of vinegar.
✴ Replace 1 tablespoon of the vinegar with wine.
✴ Add 1–2 tablespoons Dijon mustard to the vinegar before whisking in the oil.
✴ Add 1 crushed garlic clove before whisking in the oil.

Seafood salad with garlic mayonnaise.

FOOD

PREPARATION

Cooking is far easier when you are familiar with the basic techniques and preparation tips that the professionals employ, and there are plenty of time-saving methods to learn.

FISH AND SEAFOOD

SCALING OR DESCALING FISH

Some fish, such as salmon, have scales which have to be removed before cooking. This is done by holding the fish firmly at the tail end and using a knife to scrape off the scales towards the head. Rinse well under cold running water.

TRIMMING FISH

To trim round fish, use a pair of heavy scissors to cut away the fins on either side of the fish then cut away the belly fins. Cut away the dorsal fins along the back. Trim the tail by cutting a 'V' shape into it. To trim flat fish, use scissors to trim off the outer half of the small fin bones all around the fish.

SKINNING FISH FILLETS

Place the fillet, skin side down, on a board and make a small cut across the flesh at the tail end. Cut down as far as the skin but not through it. Hold the knife at an acute angle and use a sawing action to cut the flesh off the skin.

TIPS FOR HANDLING FISH

✳ Scale or descale fish in the sink if possible as the scales fly off in all directions. Ideally, do this under a gently running cold tap.

✳ To get a firm grip on fish, pour a little salt into a saucer and dip your fingers in it – this will help to prevent the skin sliding from your fingers.

MEXICAN BARBECUED SALMON

Make sure the barbecue has heated up thoroughly before you start to cook. The cooking time is slightly faster than grilling.

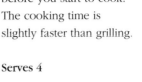

Serves 4

INGREDIENTS
1 small red onion
1 garlic clove
6 plum tomatoes
25g/1oz/2 tbsp butter
45ml/3 tbsp tomato ketchup
30ml/2 tbsp Dijon mustard
30ml/2 tbsp soft dark brown sugar
15ml/1 tbsp clear honey
1.5ml/¼ tsp ground cayenne pepper (optional)
15ml/1 tbsp chilli powder
15ml/1 tbsp ground paprika
15ml/1 tbsp Worcestershire sauce
4 x 175g/6oz salmon fillets

Chop the red onion and finely dice the garlic. Dice the tomatoes. Melt the butter in a large, heavy-based saucepan and cook the onion and garlic until clear. Add the tomatoes and simmer for 15 minutes. Add the remaining ingredients, except the salmon, and simmer for 20 minutes. Blend the mixture in a food processor fitted with a metal blade and leave to cool. Brush the salmon with the sauce and chill for at least 2 hours. Barbecue or grill for about 3–4 minutes either side, brushing on the sauce when necessary.

SEAFOOD

CLEANING MUSSELS, COCKLES AND CLAMS

Use a stiff brush to scrub the shells, scraping off any barnacles and dirt. Discard any broken or open shells. Mussels have black hairy protrusions (known as beards)  protruding from their shells – scrape and pull these away. Rinse the shellfish well before cooking.

PEELING RAW PRAWNS

Holding the prawn firmly in one hand, pull off the legs with the fingers of the other hand. Remove the head but ensure that the tail is left intact.

Loosen the shell by pressing it out sideways underneath the body where the legs have been removed, then pull it away neatly in one piece, leaving the tail in place. Pull the tail off separately if this is required.

Bouillabaisse *is a delicious Mediterranean fish stew. There are lots of variations – almost any combination of fish and shellfish can be used.*

SHELLFISH TIPS

* Live mussels, cockles and clams should have firmly closed shells. Tap any open shells – if they do not shut, discard the shellfish.
* When the shellfish are cooked, their shells should open. Discard any unopened shells.
* Avoid overcooking delicate shellfish. Scallops, mussels and prawns become tough and leathery if they are cooked for too long or at too high a temperature.

Serve one lobster per person as a main course or half a lobster per person for a starter.

LOBSTER AND CRAB

There are two classic methods of killing a large, live lobster. The first is to immerse the shellfish in a large pan of rapidly boiling water. To carry out this method successfully, you need a really big stockpot which allows plenty of room for the water to boil, and a close-fitting lid. The shellfish should be plunged smartly into the pan and the lid slammed down immediately, with the heat on the highest setting to bring the water quickly back to the boil. The shellfish will die in a couple of seconds. Crab is very often killed in this way too.

The second method is to use a large, sharp cook's knife. You need to plunge the knife right into the dark cross-shaped mark behind the head of a lobster. It is best to do this on a large, heavy board.

The alternative method is to place the live crab or lobster in a plastic carrier bag. Loosely tie the bag and put it in the freezer for several hours. This is a more humane way to kill shellfish.

CLEANING SQUID

This is not difficult to do, but it is slightly messy. Cover the surface with newspaper topped with a sheet of greaseproof paper. Grasp the tentacles and head part, then pull both firmly away from the white body sac. Cut off and keep the tentacles, which may be cut up and cooked. Discard the head.

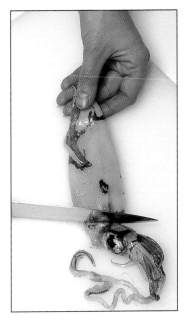

Remove the clear, plastic-like strip that runs down inside the length of the body sac. Then sprinkle a little salt on the mottled outside of the sac and use the abrasive salt to rub off the fine covering of dark skin. Rinse well. Be careful not to overcook the fish as it becomes tough very quickly.

DELICIOUS SQUID

Chop up the tentacles and sauté them with a finely chopped onion. Then mix with chopped mushrooms, breadcrumbs, grated lemon rind and chopped parsley to make a stuffing for the body sac. Do not fill the sac too full because the stuffing will expand when cooked. Secure the sac with a wooden cocktail stick. Sauté, then braise in tomato sauce. Slice the body sac into rings, toss in seasoned flour and sauté in garlic butter. Serve on a salad base and dust lightly with Parmesan cheese.

PREPARING POULTRY AND GAME

TO SPATCHCOCK A BIRD

Place the bird breast side down on a board and cut it in half along the backbone. Cut along the other side of the bone and remove it. Turn the bird over

and flatten the breast by pressing it firmly with the heel of your hand. Fold the wing ends neatly underneath and thread two long metal skewers through the bird to keep it flat. Push one skewer through the wings, keeping the breast meat flat, and another through the thighs and breast.

POULTRY AND GAME-BIRD TIPS

✳ Loosen the skin covering the breast of a bird by first snipping between it and the flesh at the vent end, then slide a small spoon or your fingers between the skin and meat. Fill with stuffing or insert knobs of herb, garlic or lemon butter between the skin and meat to prevent the meat from drying out during roasting.

✳ To check that poultry is cooked, insert the point of a skewer: juices should run clear without any sign of blood.

Push skewer into thickest part.

KITCHEN HYGIENE

Wash your hands, utensils, board and surfaces very well after handling raw fish, poultry and meat.

ROASTING A CHICKEN

Preheat the oven to 190°C/375°F/Gas 5. Remove all packaging from the cavity of the bird. Wash the chicken and pat dry. Season the inside of the chicken with salt and freshly ground black pepper and stuff if required. Truss the chicken and spread butter or lard on the breast.

Set the bird breast up on a rack in a roasting tin and season all over.

Roast the bird, basting it every 10 minutes after the first 30 minutes. If the chicken is browning too quickly it may be covered loosely with foil.

COOKING TIMES

Allow 20 minutes per ½kg/1lb plus 20 minutes added to the total cooking time. Remember to weigh the chicken after stuffing then calculate the times.

ESTIMATED ROASTING TIMES
Poussin
450–500g/1–1¼lb – roast for 40–45 minutes
Double Poussin
800–900g/1¾lb–2lb – roast for 55–50 minutes
Spring Chicken
900–1.25kg/2–2½lb – roast for 1–1¼ hours
Roaster
1.5–2kg/3–4½lb – roast for 1 hour 20/40 minutes
Boiler
2–3 kg/4½–6½lb – roast for 2–3 hours

PREPARING MEAT

You can buy meat already prepared for cooking from butchers and supermarkets but some cuts will need further preparation.

Beating steaks or thick slices of meat with a meat mallet helps to tenderize them.

✻ Lean slices of lamb, pork or braising steak can be beaten out thinly between pieces of greaseproof paper or clear film, then topped with filling and rolled.

✻ Marinating is soaking meat in a moist seasoning mixture to flavour and help tenderize it. Try it with joints, small cuts and cubed meat. Leave in the fridge for several hours, overnight or up to 2 days.

✻ Long slow cooking is best for tough cuts and for sauces made with minced meat.

✻ For large joints of meat that contain rib bones it is a good idea to cut the chine bone (backbone) where it is joined to the rib bones, to loosen it or remove it completely before cooking.

✻ Larding is when strips of fat or fatty pork or bacon are threaded through holes pierced in lean meat with a skewer.

TO BARD A JOINT

If a very lean piece of meat is to be roasted without a protective crust (a spice mixture, oil and crumbs or pastry, for example), it is a good idea to bard it to keep it moist. Wrap very thin slices of beef fat, pork fat or blanched bacon around the joint and tie them in place. Discard the fat before serving but keep the bacon, if liked.

MINCING MEAT

Minced meats of most kinds are easily obtainable, but when you want something unusual you will need to mince it yourself. Also, if minced meat is to be served raw, as in steak *tartare*, it must be freshly prepared. Trim the meat carefully (be sure to remove all gristle because a food processor will chop gristle too) and cut it into cubes. Place in a food processor fitted with the metal blade and pulse until coarse or fine.

PREPARING VEGETABLES

GRIT-FREE LEEKS

There are two ways of cleaning
leeks. Trim and three-quarters
slit a leek lengthways. Hold it
open under cold running water
until clean. Shake off the water

and slice. Or, trim, slice and separate the slices into
rings, then wash well in a colander and drain.

PEELING TOMATOES

For one or two tomatoes,
skewer them individually on a
metal fork and rotate in a gas
flame until blistered, then slide
off the skin in cold water.

Alternatively, cut a cross in the base of each tomato,
cover with freshly boiling water, leave to stand for
30–60 seconds (ripe fruit sheds its skin more quickly),
then drain. The skin will peel off easily.

ROASTING AND PEELING PEPPERS

Char the peppers under the grill
until the skin is blackened and
blistered in places, turning
occasionally. Alternatively, this
may be done over a gas flame.

Put the charred peppers in a
polythene bag, twist the top closed and leave for 5

minutes, or until cool enough
to handle. The steam loosens
the skin which can be scraped
off with a knife. Or, simply
scrape off the skin in cold
water without leaving in a bag.

GLOBE ARTICHOKES

Cut off the pointed top about
one-third of the way down.
Snip off the pointed end of
each large outside leaf. Open
up the leaves and rinse
thoroughly between them.

To remove the bottoms, break off all the coarse
outer leaves down to the pale inner leaves. Scrape off
the fuzzy centre, or "choke", (or do this after cooking)
and peel away all the leaves with a stainless steel
knife, leaving just the edible base or bottom.

ASPARAGUS

If the asparagus is young and
tender you need do no more
than trim off the ends of the
stalks. However, larger spears,
with stalk ends that are tough

and woody, need to have their skins removed. Lay a
spear flat and hold it just below the tip. Shave off the
skin with a vegetable peeler, rolling the spear as you
go to remove the skin from all sides.

FRESH SWEETCORN

Just before cooking, strip off the husks and pull off all
the silk. Trim the stalk so it is level with the base.
To remove the
kernels, use a
sharp knife to
cut them length-
ways, several
rows at a time,
from the cob.

Tempting Ideas for Vegetables

Young seasonal vegetables need no dressing up, but the abundance of vegetables available today offers the opportunity to try your hand at more creative preparations as well as simple ones.

Vegetable Variations

✴ Next time you want to use about half a large Savoy cabbage, scoop out the middle, leaving a neat cabbage shell. Then make your next meal a stuffed cabbage, filling the hollowed cabbage with a meat or rice stuffing. Enclose the cabbage and its stuffing in foil and steam it over boiling water for about 40 minutes.

✴ Stir-fry mixed vegetables to fill pancakes, roll them neatly and place in a gratin dish. Coat with cheese sauce and grill until browned.

✴ Make a delicious hot-and-cold salad by serving grilled peppers, aubergine slices and mushrooms tossed with mixed salad leaves. Sprinkle generously with freshly grated or shaved Parmesan cheese and snipped chives, and serve with soured cream.

✴ Make a vegetable stuffing for blanched cabbage leaves or red pepper halves by mashing cooked potatoes and carrots, then mixing in chopped spring onion and crumbled blue cheese, such as Stilton. A crushed garlic clove may be added if wished. Fill and bake the cabbage leaves or peppers in the usual way and serve with tomato sauce.

✴ Grilled aubergine makes an unusual sandwich filling. Cut the aubergine in half lengthways and slice into chunks. Lay the slices on a foil-covered grill and brush with oil. Grill for 10 minutes, turning and brushing with oil once. Once the slices are tender and well browned, use as a sandwich filling with garlic mayonnaise and tomatoes.

Stuffed Jacket-baked Potatoes

Cut baked potatoes in half and scoop out the centres, leaving a thin wall of flesh. Mash the scooped-out flesh with a little butter and 3 tablespoons of grated Cheddar cheese and diced cooked ham for each potato. Season to taste. Fill the potato shells with the mixture. Sprinkle the tops with grated Cheddar, then bake at 200°C/400°F/Gas 6 for 10–15 minutes.

Cauliflower Cheese

Cut a large cauliflower into florets and steam until just tender. Spread in a buttered gratin dish and scatter over 75g/3oz/1 cup sliced, sautéed mushrooms. Pour 600ml/1 pint/2½ cups cheese sauce evenly over the top and sprinkle with a mixture of grated Cheddar and fine breadcrumbs. Brown under the grill. (Serves 4)

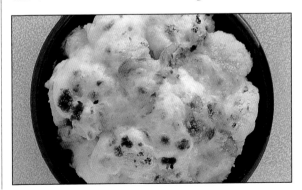

PREPARING FRUIT

Currants

Red and blackcurrants are easily removed from their stalks by scraping them off with a fork, holding the stems firmly over a bowl.

Dates

Split fresh dates and their stones come out easily. Rub off the papery skins which can be unpleasant and tough, then slice the dates and add them to salads.

Mango

Peel the fruit, then cut in as far as the stone. Now make a second cut at an angle to remove one slice. Continue slicing the fruit off the stone.

Or, cut a slice from each side, keeping close to the stone. Then score the flesh without cutting the skin and push the fruit out into a hedgehog-like shape.

Orange

To remove peel and pith, cut both ends off, then stand the fruit on a board and cut off the peel from top to bottom in thick slices all the

way around. To remove each segment, slice between the membranes and scrape out the wedges of flesh. Do this over a bowl to catch and save the juice.

Papaya

Halve the fruit to reveal small shiny black seeds. These are edible, but there are too many to be appetizing. Scoop them out and save a

few to add crunch to a salad. Peel and slice the fruit.

Cherries

Cherry stones are not difficult to remove but use a cherry stoner for the neatest presentation.

Pineapple

Cut the top and bottom off the pineapple, then sparingly slice off the spiny skin. What remains of the spines are arranged in spirals

running around the fruit. Make neat 'V' cuts to remove the spines. Slice the pineapple, then stack the slices and replace the leafy top for serving.

Citrus Fruit and Melon

Vandyking is a useful way of halving citrus fruit and melons. Use a thin-bladed, pointed knife and make an angled cut in as far as the

middle of the fruit. Work neatly all around the outside of the fruit alternating the angles of the cuts to make a 'V' shaped pattern as you cut the fruit in half. Pull the halves apart to expose the decorative serrated cuts.

Cutting Fruit

Apple and Quinces

For rings, remove the core and seeds with an apple corer. Set the fruit on its side and cut across into thick or thin rings as required.

For slices, cut the fruit in half and remove the core and seeds with a melon baller. Set one half cut side down and cut it across into neat slices, thick or thin according to recipe directions.

Pear

For "fans" cut the fruit in half and remove the core and seeds with a melon baller. Set one half cut side down and cut lengthways into thin

slices, not cutting all the way through at the stalk end. Gently spread out the slices so they are overlapping each other evenly in a decorative fan shape.

Citrus Fruit

For slices, using a serrated knife, cut the fruit across into neat slices.

For segments, hold the peeled fruit in your cupped palm. Working from the side

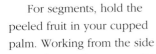

of the fruit to the centre, slide the knife down one side of a separating membrane to free the flesh from it. Then slide the knife down the other side of that segment. Drop the segment into the bowl. Continue cutting out the segments, folding back the membrane like the pages of a book.

Papaya, Avocado

For slices, cut the fruit in half and remove the seed or stone. Place each half cut side down and cut in neat slices to the thickness

required. Alternatively, cut the unpeeled fruit into wedges removing the central seeds or stone. Set each wedge peel side down and slice the knife down the length to cut the flesh away from the peel.

Melon

For slices, follow the papaya technique. For balls, use a melon baller.

Peach, Nectarine, Apricot, Plum

For slices, follow apple technique. If they need peeling first, plunge in hot water for 10-30 seconds.

Pineapple

For spears, cut the peeled fruit lengthways in half and then into quarters. Cut each quarter into spears and cut out the core. For chunks, cut the peeled fruit into spears. Remove the core. Cut across each spear into chunks. For rings, cut the peeled fruit across into slices. Stamp out the central core from each slice using a pastry cutter.

HERBS

TIPS FOR USING HERBS

✳ Put parsley sprig tops in a mug of water and snip them with scissors as required.

✳ Sprinkle a little granulated sugar over mint so it can be chopped more easily.

✳ Frozen mint leaves break up easily when crushed, so freeze whole sprigs and crush off the leaves by hand as required.

✳ Keep the flavour of fresh herbs by creaming them with butter and seasoning in a food processor or mortar. Transfer to ramekins and chill for immediate use. Or, spoon the butter on to greaseproof paper, roll into a log shape and freeze for a few of hours. Unroll, cut into slices and keep in a plastic bag in the freezer. Use within two months for the best flavour.

✳ Harvest fresh herbs before they flower.

Both fresh and dried herbs enhance the flavour of most dishes.

LEMON HERB MIX

This combination of lemon flavours makes a wonderful flavouring for chicken, to be rubbed on to the skin about one hour before roasting or barbecuing.

Makes about 50g/2oz/½ cup

INGREDIENTS
grated rind of 2 lemons
30ml/2 tbsp lemon thyme, chopped
15ml/1 tbsp lemon verbena, chopped
15ml/1 tbsp lemon grass, chopped

Peel the lemon rind to make strips and air dry the rind on a rack. Dry the herbs on kitchen paper. When everything is dry, powder using a mortar and pestel.

HERB BUTTER

A pat of flavoured butter melted over freshly cooked vegetables, meat or seafood is a perfect finishing touch.

INGREDIENTS
115g/4oz butter
30–60ml/2–4 tbsp parsley or basil
salt and pepper

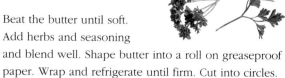

Beat the butter until soft. Add herbs and seasoning and blend well. Shape butter into a roll on greaseproof paper. Wrap and refrigerate until firm. Cut into circles.

SPICES

Tips for Using Spices

* Fresh root ginger can be prepared in several ways. Unpeeled slices can be added to some dishes. Peel and thinly slice the root, then cut it into fine shreds or sticks. Cut across the sticks for tiny dice. Grate the unpeeled root on the coarse blade of a grater, discarding the last lump of skin and fibres. Peel the root first for finer results.

* Slit fresh chillies and scrape out their seeds, then rinse well and slice or chop. Wash your hands carefully after handling chillies as their juices are extremely irritating to the skin.

* To extract all the flavour and colour from saffron, pound the threads in a mortar, then stir in a little hot water. Simply soaking the threads does not extract the most flavour and colour.

* Spices freeze well. Ground or whole, simply pack them in airtight bags and place in a tightly covered freezer container. This is a good way of storing a large batch of your favourite roasted, ground spice mix.

Spices give food a distinctive character.

Indian-Style Spice Mix

Use to make spicy stews or aromatic grills, roasts and bakes. Crushed garlic cloves and chopped fresh root ginger complement these spices.

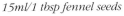

Makes about 200g/7oz/1¾ cups

Ingredients

*90ml/6 tbsp
 coriander seeds
60ml/4 tbsp cumin
 seeds
15ml/1 tbsp fennel seeds
10 green cardamoms
1 cinnamon stick
1 bay leaf
2.5ml/½ tsp turmeric
1.5ml/¼ tsp chilli powder (optional)*

Place the coriander, cumin and fennel seeds in a small saucepan. Split the cardamoms and scrape the small black seeds into the pan, then discard the shell.

Add the cinnamon and bay leaf, then dry-roast the spices over a medium heat, shaking the pan or stirring often, until the seeds are aromatic and very lightly browned. Cool slightly.

Grind the roasted spices to a powder, then mix in the turmeric and chilli powder, if used.

COOKING
METHODS

A simple cooking procedure plus the perfect ingredients equals a winning formula. This section includes tips for success with different techniques, so that you will always be able to match the method to the meal and ingredients.

METHODS OF COOKING

BOILING
Cooking rapidly in boiling liquid, either covered or uncovered. Salt is often added when using water.

SIMMERING
Cooking in liquid just below boiling point. It should shiver with the occasional bubble breaking the surface.

STEAMING
Cooking food over a pan of steadily boiling water, in a perforated container or on a plate.

STEWING
Slow cooking with liquid, in a covered pan or casserole, in the oven or on the hob. Ideal for meat.

BRAISING
Slow cooking, in the oven or on the hob, using slightly less liquid than stewing. Pan or casserole is usually covered.

SHALLOW-FRYING
Cooking in a little fat in a shallow pan, on the hob. Uses a lot less fat than deep-frying so is generally healthier.

STIR-FRYING
Frying in minimum fat over a high heat, stirring continuously. Stir-frying is usually done quickly.

DEEP-FRYING
Cooking foods submerged in fat, on the hob. A deep pan is vital as the fat bubbles up when food is added.

ROASTING
Cooking on a rack or spit in an oven; the term is also used when cooking in an uncovered tin.

POT-ROASTING
Cooking, in the oven, with a little fat, on a base of vegetables covered in a small amount of liquid.

BAKING
Cooking in the oven, covered or uncovered. The oven should be preheated to the required temperature.

GRILLING
Cooking quickly under radiant heat – used for tender foods. Barbecuing is basically the same as grilling.

BOILING AND POACHING

* Boil dried beans rapidly for 10 minutes to kill the natural toxins which are found in some beans.

* Never add salt or use salted stock when boiling dried beans: salt prevents them from becoming tender. Add the salt when the beans are cooked.

* Add a little oil when boiling pasta to prevent the water from boiling over by dispersing froth from the surface. Oil also helps to prevent pasta from sticking together when drained.

* To simmer, first bring liquid just to the boil, reduce the heat immediately and regulate it so that the liquid simmers evenly, bubbling occasionally.

Above: Swede takes about 15 minutes to cook. Do not overcook or it will be watery.

Left: Add enough liquid to come two-thirds of the way up the side of the fish.

* Poaching is more gentle than simmering, and the liquid should reach no more than simmering point at first. This method of cooking is good for fish, eggs and scallops, which toughen when boiled.

COOKING PASTA

Both fresh and dry pasta are cooked in the same way. The golden rules for success are: use plenty of water and keep checking the pasta to be sure it does not overcook. Fresh pasta will cook much more quickly than dried, it takes 1–4 minutes rather than 5 minutes.

Bring a very large pot of salted water to the boil: use at least 3½ litres/6 pints/ 15 cups of water and 2 teaspoons of salt to 450g/1lb of pasta. Drop in the pasta all at once and stir to separate the shapes or strands.

Gently push spaghetti into the pan.

If you are cooking spaghetti allow the ends in the water to soften slightly and then gently push in the rest as soon as you can.

Bring the water back to the boil, then reduce the heat slightly and boil until the pasta is just done. For dried pasta, follow the packet instructions, but start testing as soon as you reach the minimum time given. To test, lift a piece of pasta out on a wooden fork or slotted spoon. Cut it in half, there should be no sign of opaque uncooked pasta in the centre. Or bite it – it should be tender but still firm. In Italian, this is when it is '*al dente*' – to the tooth.

Drain the pasta well in a colander, shaking it vigorously to remove all excess water. Serve immediately because the pasta will continue to cook from its own heat.

BOILING AND POACHING EGGS

✳ Bring eggs to room temperature before boiling them to prevent the shells from cracking.

✳ For soft-boiled eggs, lower the eggs into simmering water, bring rapidly back to the boil and cook for 3–4 minutes, depending on how firm you like the white to be.

✳ For hard-boiled eggs, heat the eggs gently in cold water until boiling,

Lower eggs into boiling water.

then time them for 10 minutes. For a slightly moist (not floury) yolk, allow 8 minutes.

✳ Quickly sprinkle salt into the cooking water if an egg cracks while it is boiling – this sets the white quickly and helps to prevent the egg from spilling out.

✳ To poach an egg, bring a shallow pan of water to the boil, adding a little vinegar. A frying pan is ideal. Swirl the water with a spoon and drop the egg into the centre of the swirl – this will give it a good shape. Control the heat so that the water is barely

Lift out the poached egg carefully with a slotted spoon.

simmering and baste the egg occasionally.

✳ Use a slotted spoon to drain the poached egg well, then trim off the straggly bits of white with a pair of kitchen scissors or a sharp knife.

✳ Adding a drop of vinegar to the cooking water will help to set the white quickly.

STEAMING

✳ Boil water steadily to produce enough steam for cooking. Have a kettle of boiling water ready to top it up when steaming for a long time.

✳ Add herbs, such as rosemary, bay or thyme, to the water when steaming vegetables.

Steaming helps retain the colour and flavour of foods.

✳ Season small portions of fish or chicken with grated lemon rind and chopped tarragon, then wrap in spinach leaves before steaming.

A combination of greaseproof paper and foil is the best way to cover steamed puddings.

✳ Use greased greaseproof paper and foil to cover steamed puddings. Make a pleat in the covering so that it has room to expand when the pudding rises.

✳ Fold a thick band of foil long enough to lower basins or dishes into a steamer. Stand the container on the band of foil, lower it into the steamer, then fold the ends of the foil over the top, ready for lifting the dish out again when the food is cooked.

Casserole Ideas

* For fish and seafood casseroles, cook onions and other vegetables well (with stock, wine and/or canned tomatoes) before adding the fish. This way, all the ingredients will be cooked to

Cooking a seafood casserole.

perfection and the seafood will not be overcooked.

* Brown meat well first for a richly coloured and flavoured casserole.

* Sweat onions or leeks with garlic (if liked) in a little butter or olive oil as the base for a vegetable casserole. Stir the onions or leeks to coat them in the hot fat, then cover and cook gently for 10–15 minutes, until they have softened but not coloured.

* Make a one-pot meal by adding rice or pasta shapes (elbow macaroni, bows and small shells are good) for the final 30–40 minutes cooking – delicious with meat or poultry. Ensure that there is plenty of sauce and that the pot is closely covered. Cook in the oven or over a low heat, allowing longer than is usual for pasta as the liquid is not boiling.

* Add plenty of chopped parsley before serving a casserole for a contrasting flavour and colour. Mint, coriander and dill are also suitable; grated lemon rind, finely chopped garlic and parsley make a classic addition for *osso bucco* (veal stew) and are also excellent with lamb or pork.

Casseroles make hearty meals.

Lamb Stew with Peas

This stew is cooked for a relatively long time, producing tender, tasty meat.

Serves 4-6

INGREDIENTS

900g–1.2kg/2–2¹/₂lbs boned lamb shoulder, trimmed of excess fat and cut into 4cm/1¹/₂in cubes
450ml/³/₄ pint/1⁷/₈ cups lamb or chicken stock
1 onion, chopped
15ml/1 tbsp chopped fresh rosemary or 5ml/1 tsp crumbled dried rosemary
salt and pepper
300g/11oz frozen peas, thawed and drained
15ml/1 tbsp mint jelly

Put the lamb and 120ml/4fl oz/¹/₂ cup stock in a casserole, cover and cook over a low heat for about 30 minutes. Remove the lid and boil the juices, stirring, until reduced to a sticky glaze. Brown the meat evenly. Remove the lamb with a slotted spoon and set aside.

Skim the juices to remove the fat and add another 120ml/4 fl oz/¹/₂ cup stock. Boil and stir well. Add the onion and rosemary and cook until the onion is soft. Return the lamb to the casserole with the rest of the stock and season. Boil, cover and simmer for about 1 hour.

Lift out the lamb and keep warm. Skim the fat from the liquid. Add the peas; simmer for 2 minutes. Add the mint jelly and stir in the lamb cubes. Serve hot.

CASSEROLE ADDITIONS

✱ When making slowly simmered poultry casseroles or long-cooked meat stews, it is better to use water when vegetables are added for flavour than to use a stock cube or powder which may well overpower the casserole.

✱ Unsweetened apple juice is delicious in pork, gammon, bacon or lamb stews.

✱ Add a pinch of sugar when using canned tomatoes or a large quantity of fresh tomatoes as this counteracts their sharpness.

✱ Medium-dry cider is a good substitute for wine in everyday casseroles and stews.

✱ A little dry sherry enlivens poultry casseroles. Be sure to cook it for at least 15 minutes to take away the 'raw alcohol' flavour.

COMPLEMENTARY FINISHING TOUCHES

✱ A crusty topping of sliced French bread spread with butter and mustard is delicious on meat, poultry and game stews. Alternatively, place grated cheese on top and float on French onion soup for a tasty snack or starter.

✱ Swirls of soured cream or plain yogurt provide a pleasing contrast to rich sauces in meat stews.

✱ Crisp *croûtons* of bread make a crunchy garnish for thinly sauced fish, seafood and poultry casseroles.

✱ A crunchy breadcrumb topping gives a vegetable casserole a pleasing texture. Sprinkle with cheese before baking to add flavour.

✱ Snipped chives or your favourite herbs make a decorative finish.

A tasty casserole with a generous helping of creamy potato makes a special treat.

Sliced French bread, topped with mustard and cheese, is a great addition to onion soup.

FRYING TECHNIQUES

COATINGS

* Seasoned flour readily clings to damp food and forms a light coating when cooked.
* Egg and breadcrumbs provide a thicker coating than flour. Coat the food in seasoned flour, then dip it in beaten egg and coat thoroughly with fine, dry white breadcrumbs.

Frying breaded fish.

* A double egg and breadcrumb coating can be an effective protection for delicate foods.
* Batter can be used: coat the food in flour first so that the batter clings to it and stays on during cooking.

FRYING TIPS

* The fat must be hot before adding food. This quickly cooks the outside so that the result is crisp, not greasy.
* Fry only a few pieces of food at a time.
* Drain the food well over the pan, then on kitchen paper to absorb any excess oil.
* Serve fried food freshly cooked.

STIR-FRY RULES

* Use a large pan, preferably a wok, so that the food can be stirred easily.
* Use a small amount of oil that withstands high heat, such as groundnut or sunflower. Olive oil burns too quickly.

Stir-fried vegetables.

* Make sure that all ingredients are cut into small, even-sized pieces before cooking.
* Cook items which take longest first, then add foods which cook quickly towards the end.

THE ULTIMATE FISH AND CHIPS

This batter is light and crisp and the standing time is an essential factor. Do not peel the potatoes as the peel contains nutrients and gives a crispier crunch.

Serves 4

INGREDIENTS
*115g/4oz/1 cup
    plain flour
15ml/1 tbsp olive oil
2 eggs, separated
30ml/2 tbsp chopped
    fresh herbs
vegetable oil, for
    deep frying
4 x 175g/6oz cod
    fillets
8 large waxy potatoes
salt and ground black pepper*

Sift the flour and seasoning into a large mixing bowl. Whisk the olive oil with 120ml/4fl oz/½ cup water and the egg yolks to make a smooth batter. Stir in the mixed herbs and leave to stand for at least 30 minutes.

Whisk the egg whites until stiff and fold into the mixture. Heat the oil in a large, heavy-based saucepan – test the heat with a piece of stale bread, it should sizzle instantly. Coat the fish fillets in batter and deep-fry for 4–7 minutes until golden brown. Drain well on kitchen paper and keep hot.

Meanwhile, make the chips. Cut the unpeeled potatoes into wedges and deep-fry for 10 minutes until golden brown and crisp.

FATS FOR FRYING

Butter

Butter is often served with food or used as a basis for a sauce. Clarified butter is best for cooking as the solids which tend to burn have been removed and the water content has evaporated.

TO MAKE CLARIFIED BUTTER

Melt the butter in a saucepan and heat gently until a white sediment forms in the bottom of the pan. Remove from the heat, pour the clear yellow fat into a bowl or jug and discard the milky residue.

Ghee

This is clarified butter used in Indian cooking.

Lard

This is clarified pork fat which can be used for shallow- or deep-frying.

Dripping

This is taken from meat and can be the fat rendered from a joint when cooking, then strained.

Vegetable Oil

This is a mixture of different vegetable oils. Suitable for shallow- or deep-frying.

Cooking Oil

This usually includes fish oils as well as vegetable oils, so it is avoided by vegetarians.

Groundnut Oil

This has a high smoking point, so it is useful for deep-frying at a high temperature.

Sesame Oil

Used in small quantities to flavour another oil (often groundnut) used for stir-frying. Sesame oil smokes and burns at a low temperature.

Corn Oil

This can be heated to a high temperature before it smokes and breaks down, so it is useful for deep- and shallow-frying.

Sunflower Oil

A good standard oil which can be used for frying or salad dressings.

Olive Oil

This smokes at a comparatively low temperature and is not suitable for deep-frying. It can be dangerous as a medium for deep-frying unless it is closely watched and the temperature controlled to prevent the oil from overheating.

Oils come in many flavours.

Bottled oils keep for a long time.

A selection of solid fats – butter, lard, suet and margarine.

ROASTING CHART

	TEMPERATURE	TIME
Chicken	200°C/400°F/Gas 6	20 minutes per 450g/1lb, plus 20 minutes
Turkey	180°C/350°F/Gas 4	For birds up to 4.5kg/10lb: 20 minutes per 450g/1lb, plus 20 minutes
		For birds over 4.5kg/10lb: 15 minutes per 450g/1lb, plus 15 minutes
Large turkey	160°C/325°F/Gas 3	For birds over 6.8kg/15lb: 20 minutes per 450g/1lb, plus 20 minutes
		For birds over 9kg/20lb: about 30 minutes per 450g/1lb (turn and check bird regularly)
Beef	220°C/425°F/Gas 7	15–20 minutes per 450g/1lb, plus 15–20 minutes
	180°C/350°F/Gas 4	20–30 minutes per 450g/1lb, plus 20–30 minutes
Lamb	190°C/375°F/Gas 5	20–30 minutes per 450g/1lb, plus 20–30 minutes
	180°C/350°F/Gas 4	20–35 minutes per 450g/1lb, plus 20–35 minutes
Pork	180°C/350°F/Gas 4	30–35 minutes per 450g/1lb, plus 30–35 minutes

USING A MEAT THERMOMETER

Insert the thermometer so that its tip is in the middle of the thick meat. The temperature of the meat indicates the extent to which it is cooked.

Beef	rare	60°C/140°F
	medium	70°C/158°F
	well done	80°C/176°F
Lamb	medium	70–75°C/158–167°F
	well done	75–80°C/167–176°F
Pork	well done	80–85°C/176–185°F

Cooked to perfection, turkey is a real treat.

PREPARING MEAT FOR ROASTING

TO TIE A BONED JOINT

Joints that have been boned should be tied into a neat shape for roasting or pot-roasting. The butcher will do this, but if you want to add a

stuffing or seasoning you will need to retie the joint yourself. Reshape it into a neat roll that is even in circumference. Use butchers' string to make ties around the circumference of the joint at 2.5cm/1in intervals.

PREPARING A LEG OF LAMB

According to the recipe, rub the joint with oil or butter and season. If wished, for extra flavour, with the tip of a sharp knife make little slits in

the meat all over the surface, then insert flavouring such as herbs, slivers of garlic, olive slices, shards of fresh ginger and so on. Roast for the suggested time, basting if necessary.

STUFFING A CHICKEN

Only stuff the small neck-end of the chicken and not the large cavity inside the carcass, as the heat from the oven will not penetrate all the way through the chicken.

TRUSSING A CHICKEN

Fold the flap of neck skin underneath and tuck the wing tips (pinions) back and under the chicken. Turn the bird on its back, press the legs down into its sides to give

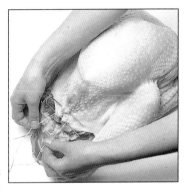

the breast a good plump shape. Thread a trussing needle (a 25cm/10in needle) with fine string, long enough to thread through the bird and back again.

Insert the trussing needle through the wing joint, between the two small bones, and then through the body to emerge in the same position on the other side. Re-insert the needle into the other end of the wing joint (making a long stitch) and pass the needle back through the body and out at the same position of the opposite wing joint. Tie the two pieces of string together. Re-thread the trussing needle and insert it through the drumstick next to the joint on the leg, and through the body cavity to the opposite leg. Insert back through the lower end of the drumsticks and tie the two thread ends. Turn the bird to bring the string up to tie the drumsticks and parson's nose together.

STUFFING TIPS

* The stuffing should be cool, not hot or chilled.
* Pack the stuffing loosely into the bird because it will expand during cooking.
* Cook left-over stuffing separately.

GRILLING AND BARBECUING

Foods which cook well under a grill are usually also excellent barbecue candidates. Here are a few ideas:

WHOLE VEGETABLES TO GRILL OR BARBECUE

✱ **Corn on the Cob** Fold back the husk and remove the silky fibres, then carefully replace the husk to protect the corn kernels while they are grilled. Remove the husk for serving.

✱ **Whole Peppers** Grill until blistered but not blackened, then split and remove the core and seeds. Serve with olive oil and seasoning.

✱ **Mushrooms** Large open mushrooms should be brushed with butter and grilled quickly on both sides.

✱ **Potatoes** Boil in their skins until just tender, then brush with oil or melted butter and cook until crisp and brown on the barbecue.

✱ **Courgettes** Select small courgettes and trim off their ends. Brush with oil and grill until well browned. Serve split and topped with butter.

Kebabs cook quickly on a barbecue.

SKEWER FILLERS

✱ Thinly peel courgettes, cut them into chunks and wrap in short lengths of bacon.

✱ Chunks of thick cod fillet, monkfish or whole scallops are also delicious wrapped in bacon or Parma ham and grilled.

✱ Boil new potatoes until just tender, then marinate with a little curry paste and garlic until cold. Skewer the potatoes with cloves of garlic.

✱ Wrap chunks of mango in Parma ham or thinly sliced smoked ham and brush with olive oil.

MEAT BARBECUING TIPS

✱ Trim excess fat from meat as dripping can cause dangerous flare-ups.

✱ Always make sure meat is thoroughly cooked. Test by piercing the thickest part of the flesh: juices should run clear and the flesh should not have a trace of pink.

Barbecued vegetables are delicious.

SWEET GRILLS

Grilled bananas require little preparation.

✱ Grill whole bananas until their skins are black, then serve with maple syrup and whipped cream or fromage frais.

✱ Core and halve eating apples, grill cut side down, then turn and top with brown sugar and cinnamon. Grill until bubbling and serve with Greek-style yogurt or créme fraîche.

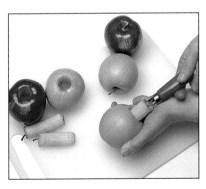

Core apples before filling or adding topping.

✱ Skewer chunks of plain cake with chunks of pineapple. Brush with melted unsalted butter and roll in desiccated coconut. Grill until golden.

CHAR-GRILLED SAUSAGES WITH PRUNES AND BACON

Sausages are a barbecue favourite and this is one way to make them a little different. With a sharp knife, cut a long slit through one side of each sausage, cutting them about three-quarters of the way through. Spread the cut surface with mustard and then place three prunes in each sausage, pressing them in firmly. Stretch the bacon rashers out thinly with the back of a knife. Wrap the bacon round the sausages, to hold them in shape. Cook over a hot barbecue for 15–18 minutes, turning occasionally until evenly browned and thoroughly cooked.

MARINATED CHICKEN

This marinade will add flavour and moisten the chicken. Place the chicken in a wide dish or bowl, preferably large enough to allow it to lie in a single layer. Mix

together crushed garlic, olive oil, dry sherry, Worcestershire sauce, soy sauce and freshly ground black pepper. Pour the marinade over the chicken and turn to coat it evenly. Cover the dish and put in the fridge for several hours, turning the chicken over occasionally and spooning the marinade over it. Remove the chicken with a slotted spoon and keep the marinade for basting or brushing the chicken during cooking.

BAKING

BAKING TEMPERATURES AND TIMES

Bread (medium loaf)
40–50 minutes at 220°C/425°F/Gas 7

Pizza (time varies according to toppings)
25–35 minutes at 220°C/425°F/Gas 7

Pastry Quiche, baking blind with paper and beans
15 minutes at 200°C/400°F/Gas 6

Pastry Quiche, with whisked egg and milk filling
45 minutes at 180°C/350°F/Gas 4

Pastry Fruit Tart (short pastry, raw fruit filling)
50 minutes at 190°C/375°F/Gas 5

Swiss Roll (or thin, oblong whisked sponge)
12–15 minutes at 220°C/425°F/Gas 7

Sandwich Cake (creamed mixture in 2 tins)
about 30 minutes at 160°C/325°F/Gas 3

Small Cakes (creamed mixture, in paper cases)
about 20 minutes at 190°C/375°F/Gas 5

BAKING EN PAPILLOTE

Portions of fish or poultry can be baked with flavourings in paper packets. Circles of greaseproof paper can be used, but non-stick baking parchment is better. Place the ingredients on one side of the paper, double it over, then fold, twist and pinch the edges to seal in the food. Cook on a baking sheet.

COOKING IN A BAIN MARIE

A bain marie can be used on the hob or in the oven. A roasting tin is ideal for small dishes of food, such as custard. Stand the dishes in the tin and pour in hot, not boiling, water until it covers two-thirds of the outsides of the dishes. The water protects delicate mixtures, such as custard, from fierce heat which curdles them.

BAKING TIPS

* Use cold and firm fat for making pastry, particularly if using a food processor. Cold fat is less likely to soften too much as it is rubbed into the flour, resulting in oily pastry.

* To stop pastry from shrinking, refrigerate the dough before rolling out and baking. This 'resting time' will allow any elasticity developed during mixing to relax.

Add the finishing touch to a pie with fruit and pastry decorations.

* Many cakes can be frozen successfully when wrapped in greaseproof paper and then foil.
* A short, sturdy drinking glass can be used as a pastry cutter. Flour the rim well and do not press too hard.
* Use easy-blend (or fast-action) yeast for bread making. Unlike ordinary yeast there is no need to mix it with liquid.

* A stoneware pizza baking brick or stone will give a pizza a very crisp crust. A flat terracotta tile will have the same result.

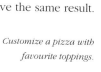

Customize a pizza with favourite toppings.

BAKING KNOW-HOW

A selection of baked goods.

CHECKING CAKES

✳ A thin creamed or whisked sponge is cooked when the top is browned, the sides have shrunk slightly from the tin and the middle feels springy when pressed gently with the fingertips.

✳ A large cake should be tested by inserting a metal skewer into its centre. If the skewer is free of sticky mixture, the cake is cooked; if there is a layer of raw mixture on the skewer, cook for a further 5 minutes.

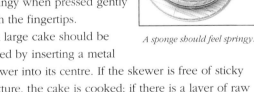

A sponge should feel springy.

CHECKING BREAD

✳ Turn the loaf over and tap the bottom – if the loaf is cooked through it will sound hollow. If the loaf sounds solid and damp, then cook for a few more minutes.

Bread should sound hollow.

PREVENTING BAKED ITEMS FROM OVERBROWNING

✳ If a cake or loaf is becoming too dark on top before it is cooked through, cut a small piece of foil and loosely cover the top. Do not tent the top completely, or tuck the foil around the container, as this would retain too much steam; drape it loosely to allow the item to bake without the crust becoming too dark.

COOLING BAKED ITEMS

✳ Soft biscuits, such as shortbread, should be left in the baking tin or on the sheet for a few minutes, until the mixture is firm enough to be transferred to a wire rack without crumbling.

✳ Cooling on a wire rack allows steam to escape and prevents breads, cakes and other baked items from developing a soggy base.

✳ Cover the cooling rack with kitchen paper or a clean dish towel when cooling a whisked sponge, otherwise the wire will mark the surface of the cake.

✳ Leave rich fruit cakes, which are baked for many hours at a low temperature, to cool in their tins. This will ensure the cake is moist and the crust will soften. Cover the tin with a dish towel and leave overnight.

Baking your own bread is cheap and easy, and the results are impressive.

MENU
MAKERS

Although the main dish is usually the central focus of the menu, the rest of the meal should not be left as an afterthought. Choose all the elements of your menu carefully to ensure a perfect balance and the meal will be a success.

THE PERFECT MENU

When entertaining, it is fun to plan a splendid menu. Here are a few points for success – the emphasis is on taste and aesthetic appeal, not nutrition. The pictures in each column illustrate a well-balanced menu.

✳ When planning two or more courses, remember that they should complement each other in flavour, texture and appearance.

✳ Serve a light starter before a substantial main course, or a small portion of a rich or hearty starter followed by a light main dish.

✳ Do not overpower the palate with flavour at first: never serve a spicy starter before a delicate main dish.

✳ If you plan a spectacular dessert – chocolate fondue, for example – make preceding courses very light, keep portions modest and let your guests know that they can expect to feast on the *finale*!

✳ It is a good idea to offer a choice of desserts – one light fruit dish or sorbet to balance richer fare, such as chocolate gâteau or creamy syllabub.

✳ A multi-course meal, with starter, fish, main dish, cheese and dessert, can be successful if portions are modest. Ensure the dishes are well matched and that the early savoury courses lead smoothly into the main course, but do make sure that each course makes a distinct statement.

A WEEKEND LUNCH

Stuffed Garlic Mushrooms.

Spanish Omelette.

Fresh Figs, Chocolate and Liqueur.

A DINNER PARTY

Melon and Parma Ham.

Dover Sole in a Parsley Jacket.

Apples in Rose Pouchong Syrup.

SAUCES FOR COURSES

Here are some speedy versions of popular, versatile sauces that will enhance many meals.

ONE-STAGE WHITE SAUCE

Place 40g/1½oz/⅓ cup plain flour in a saucepan. Gradually whisk in 600ml/1 pint/2½ cups milk. Add a pinch of ground mace, a bay leaf, knob of butter, salt and pepper. Whisk over a medium heat until boiling, then simmer for 3 minutes, whisking frequently.

Finely chop a handful of parsley and 2 hard-boiled eggs. Add to the sauce and serve with fish, pasta, boiled ham or spinach on cooked rice.

RICH MUSHROOM SAUCE

Cook 225g/8oz/2 cups sliced button mushrooms in a little butter for 10 minutes, until their juices have evaporated. Add to the One-Stage White Sauce and serve with fish, poultry, meat or pasta.

QUICK TOMATO SAUCE

Grate 1 carrot and 1 onion. Cook on the hob in 30ml/2 tbsp olive oil with 2 crushed garlic cloves and 1 bay leaf for 15 minutes, stirring often. Add 600ml/1 pint/2½ cups passata, 45ml/3 tbsp chopped parsley and salt and pepper to taste.

Boil the sauce rapidly for a couple of minutes, then lower the heat and simmer for 15 minutes.

Serve with fish, poultry or meat. For supper, serve with fresh pasta and plenty of Parmesan cheese or pour the sauce over hard-boiled eggs arranged on a bed of cooked rice, top with grated cheese and grill until browned.

Coat pasta with tomato sauce, top with poached eggs and sprinkle with grated or shaved Pecorino cheese and shredded basil.

TARTARE SAUCE

Halve 2 hard-boiled eggs, remove the yolks and press them through a sieve into a bowl. Blend in 1 raw egg yolk and mix until smooth. Stir in 10ml/2 tsp fresh lemon juice. Add 175ml/6fl oz/¾ cup olive oil very slowly, a little at a time, whisking constantly. When it begins to thicken, start to add the oil more quickly to form an emulsion.

Chop 1 egg white into fine chunks and stir into the sauce with 5ml/1 tsp each of chopped capers, gherkins, fresh chives and fresh parsley. Season with salt and pepper to taste. Serve Tartare Sauce with fried or grilled fish.

HOLLANDAISE SAUCE

Place 30ml/2 tbsp white wine vinegar in a pan with
15ml/1 tbsp water, 6 black peppercorns and 1 bay leaf.
Simmer gently until the liquid has reduced by half.
Strain and cool. Cream 115g/4oz/½ cup butter until
soft. In a double saucepan, whisk together 2 egg yolks
and the vinegar mixture until light and fluffy.

Gradually add the
butter a tiny piece at a time
– about the size of a
hazelnut will be enough.
Whisk quickly until all the
butter has been absorbed
before adding more.
Season lightly and, if the
sauce is too sharp, add a
little more butter piece by piece.

For the best result, serve immediately with fish,
poached eggs or fresh vegetables. Hollandaise Sauce is
also a delicious accompaniment for many vegetables,
including asparagus and artichokes.

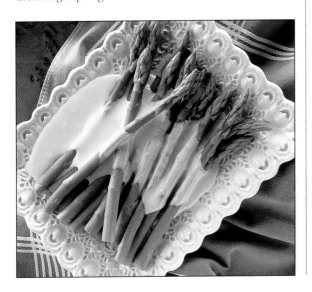

TIPS FOR SAUCES

* A food processor does not produce a completely
smooth puréed sauce (or soup, in fact) as the result is
slightly 'grainy'.

* Rescue a lumpy sauce by straining it through a sieve.
In severe cases of lumpiness, where you can't afford to
lose the lumps as they are needed to thicken the
liquid, press the sauce through a fine nylon sieve or
purée the lumps with the sauce. You may have to
forfeit the texture of other ingredients in the sauce in
order to remove the lumps.

* Beating or whisking a sauce or gravy thoroughly as it
cooks and thickens and before serving gives a good
texture and glossy sheen – this is true of sauces
thickened with flour and those enriched with butter at
the end of cooking.

* Enliven a weak-flavoured gravy by adding a *little*
tomato purée and sherry – not enough to be readily
identified, but sufficient to add interest – and simmer
for a few minutes. Also check the seasoning as the lack
of flavour could be due to insufficient salt.

* Sometimes, the sauce simply needs reducing by
boiling for a few minutes to concentrate the flavour.

RESCUE REMEDY

In desperate curdled-sauce situations, where
cream has separated or egg yolks have curdled,
strain the sauce through a fine sieve. In a clean
pan, heat some butter and stir in flour to make a
paste. Cook this for 3 minutes, stirring, but not
letting the mixture brown, then slowly stir in the
strained sauce and bring to the boil.

The result may not be as originally
intended but it will be more acceptable than
a separated sauce!

SALAD SPINNERS

* Salads of fresh, raw fruit and vegetables play a useful role in a well-balanced diet, not only as colourful, crunchy side dishes but as exciting light meals, bulky sandwich fillings and delicious baked-potato toppings.
* Well-prepared fresh ingredients and a flavoursome dressing are the keys to success with salads.
* Ingredients that discolour, such as avocados and apples, should be cut up at the last minute.
* Some ingredients benefit from being marinated for a couple of hours before serving – mushrooms, potatoes and tomatoes are good examples.
* Cut foods into similar shapes and sizes for harmony when eating – small or large slices, shreds or strips.

OIL AND VINEGAR DRESSING

Whisk 5ml/1 tsp sugar, 5ml/1 tsp mustard, a good pinch of salt and a generous grind of black pepper with 30ml/2 tbsp balsamic or cider vinegar. Whisk until the sugar and salt have dissolved. Then gradually whisk in 120ml/8 tbsp/½ cup olive oil, adding it in a slow stream. Whisk hard until the dressing is thick. Taste and add more salt or pepper if needed.

* A crushed garlic clove, chopped parsley or tarragon may be added.
* For a delicious marinade for mushrooms, tomatoes or cheese (mozzarella or feta in particular), add 15ml/ 1 tbsp roasted fennel seeds, 1 crushed garlic clove and 1 bay leaf to the oil and vinegar mixture.

PERFECT MAYONNAISE

This cold emulsified sauce of oils and egg yolks has a multitude of uses.

Makes about 350ml/12 fl oz/1½ cups

INGREDIENTS
2 egg yolks
salt and freshly ground
  pepper
2.5ml/½ tsp caster
  sugar
2.5ml/½ tsp mild
  mustard
30ml/2 tbsp lemon
  juice
250ml/8fl oz/1 cup olive oil

Put the egg yolks in a small basin. Add a good sprinkling of salt and pepper, the caster sugar, mustard and lemon juice. Add 15ml/1 tbsp oil to the mixture. Whisk up the mixture with an electric beater. Then whisking rapidly, add the oil drop by drop at first, increasing to a trickle as it is absorbed. When the mixture turns pale and thick, add more lemon juice and more seasoning to taste.

RESCUE REMEDY

If the mayonnaise curdles at any point, STOP mixing. Crack a fresh yolk into a perfectly clean bowl and add 15ml/1 tbsp of the curdled mixture. Whisk well, then slowly add the rest of the curdled mixture, whisking all the time.

With crispy French bread, Salad Niçoise makes a wonderful summer lunch or light supper.

FLAVOURING MAYONNAISE

Garlic Mayonnaise Add a crushed and finely chopped garlic clove to the yolk mixture. Serve as a dip.

Lemon and Parsley Mayonnaise Add the grated rind of 1 lemon and plenty of chopped parsley. Good with fish, seafood and chicken.

SALAD NICOISE

Made with good quality ingredients, this Provençal salad makes a simple yet unbeatable summer lunch or supper dish. Serve with crusty country-style bread and chilled white wine.

Serves 4

INGREDIENTS

115g/4oz French beans, trimmed
115g/4oz mixed salad leaves
½ small cucumber, thinly sliced
4 ripe tomatoes, quartered
200g/7oz can tuna in oil, drained
50g/2oz can anchovies, drained
4 eggs, hard-boiled
½ bunch radishes, trimmed
50g/2oz/½ cup small black olives
flat leaf parsley, to garnish

For the dressing
90ml/6tbsp extra virgin olive oil
2 garlic cloves, crushed
15ml/1 tbsp white wine vinegar
salt and ground black pepper

To make the dressing, quickly whisk the oil, garlic and vinegar together in bowl and season to taste.

Cut the French beans in half and cook in a saucepan of boiling water for 2 minutes until only just tender, then drain. Mix the salad leaves, cucumber, tomatoes and beans in a large, shallow salad bowl. Flake the tuna. Cut the anchovies in half lengthways. Shell and quarter the hard-boiled eggs.

Scatter the radishes, tuna, anchovies, eggs and olives over the salad. Pour over the dressing and toss together lightly. Serve garnished with parsley.

CONDIMENTS AND ACCOMPANIMENTS

Thanks to the wonderful international exchange of ingredients and food ideas, and the successful mingling of classic dishes from different countries, today's cook is at liberty to flaunt tradition and combine all sorts of flavours and textures in any one course. It is important, though, to appreciate the point of some of the classic combinations by sampling them and understanding why sweet and sour, sharp and rich, smooth and crunchy, or light and heavy flavours and textures complement each other.

TYPE OF DISH	ACCOMPANIMENT IDEAS
Soups	Croûtons of fried bread, garlic bread, small puff pastry shapes
Pâtés/Savoury Moulds	Hot wholemeal or granary toast, thin Melba toast (cold), warmed Bath Oliver biscuits or water biscuits, thin bread and butter, celery sticks, chicory leaves, simple salads
Smoked Fish	Horseradish cream, tartare sauce, parsley sauce, soured cream with chives, thin bread and butter
Chicken	Sage and onion or parsley and thyme stuffing, rice stuffings, bread sauce, crisp-grilled bacon rolls
Turkey	Sage and onion stuffing, chestnut stuffing, sausage meat stuffing, cranberry sauce, grilled bacon rolls, grilled sausages

Pâté served on thick slices of toast.

Smoked haddock in parsley sauce.

TYPE OF DISH	ACCOMPANIMENT IDEAS
Duck or Goose	Tart fruit jellies (such as red-currant or crab apple), apple sauce, orange sauce, apricots, plums
Beef	Horseradish sauce, mustard, Yorkshire pudding or popovers, roast parsnips
Lamb	Mint sauce, redcurrant jelly, rosemary, tart fruit (apricots or plums), mushroom stuffing, sausagemeat and herb stuffing
Pork	Apple sauce, sage and onion stuffing, tart fruit (apricots, apples, pineapple) crab apple jelly or other sharp fruit jellies
Soft/Creamy Desserts	Crisp thin biscuits, brandy snaps, almond macaroons or ratafias, contrasting tangy fruit sauces
Pastry Desserts	Cream, fromage frais, yogurt, custard sauce, hot thickened fruit sauces
Crêpes and Waffles	Lemon juice, sugar and currants, soft cheese, cream, crème fraîche, yogurt, jam, maple syrup, honey, stewed fruit, chocolate sauce, ice cream

Pork with apple sauce.

A crisp biscuit basket is perfect for ice cream.

Crêpes with orange sauce.

Planning a Balanced Diet

For a balanced diet, eat a variety of foods, with a high proportion of starch, vegetables and fruit. There is no such thing as an unhealthy food. There is nothing wrong with eating the occasional comparatively high-fat meal – as long as it is not a regular event. Here are tips for everyday good eating.

✳ Aim to eat at least five portions of fruit or vegetables a day: try fresh fruit for breakfast and at lunch, a salad, two or three portions of vegetables with the main meal and another portion of fruit for a snack.

Fruit and nuts are a healthy option. Serve on their own or with the cheese at the end of the meal. Seedless grapes are universally liked.

✳ Frozen vegetables are just as valuable if you do not have fresh ones.
✳ Rely on starchy foods as fillers: rice and other grains, pasta, potatoes, pulses and bread.
✳ It is not necessary to eat only wholemeal bread, but it is a good idea to eat at least half and half wholemeal and white bread.
✳ Breakfast cereal is a good source of fibre, but avoid cereals that have a high sugar content.

✳ If you consume a lot of milk regularly (a generous portion on cereal, in several hot drinks a day, sauces and so on), then switch to semi-skimmed or skimmed milk. This depends on how much other fat you eat.
✳ You should not eat more than 35 per cent of your calorie intake in fat. If you eat fried food and high-fat food daily or consume a high proportion in a week, you should cut down.
✳ Animal fats should not constitute more than about 10 per cent of your calorie intake.
✳ Protein is important, but when fish, poultry, meat, eggs and cheese are eaten regularly there is unlikely to be a shortage in the average diet.

Bread is a useful filler.

Healthy Tips
✳ A modest portion of fat is required for a healthy diet as it is a source of nutrients.
✳ Do not try to achieve a fat-free or virtually fat-free diet as it is not healthy – any severe diet restrictions should be adopted only on considered medical advice.
✳ Children under the age of 5 years should not have their fat intake restricted by giving them skimmed milk products or low-fat foods.

Most vegetarians enjoy a broad range of vegetables, and must eat a wide variety for balanced nutrition.

VEGETARIAN DIETS

✴ When fish, poultry and meat are excluded, other sources of protein have to be sought. Although vegetarian dishes are popular, and many people do not eat animal protein foods daily, those who are strictly vegetarian are in the minority.

✴ Lacto-vegetarians eat cheese, milk and eggs (although many do not appreciate boiled, fried or poached eggs), along with beans and pulses, grains and soya products as sources of protein. The danger in eliminating animal proteins without substituting a broad variety of vegetable foods is in relying on dairy produce for protein, so the lacto-vegetarian may eat large quantities of foods such as cheese daily and increase the fat content of his or her diet.

Dairy products are an important source of protein for vegetarians.

✴ The vegan diet is one that excludes all animal products, including dairy foods. Obtaining the right balance of amino acids, which make up the protein needed by the human body, and vitamins obtained from animal foods is not easy in a vegan diet. On the whole, a vegan diet is not recommended for children or young adults.

PERFECT
PRESENTATION

Decorative finishing touches and eye-catching garnishes will not make a bland recipe taste any better, but they will give a wonderful-tasting but plain dish the visual appeal it deserves.

SAVOURY GARNISHES

* The garnish should complement the flavour, texture and colour of food. Avoid irrelevant salad garnishes that cannot be eaten with the food; for example, frilly leaves floating on the edge of a rich gravy.

* Garnish fish dishes with fresh herbs, lemon or lime slices or wedges, pats of herb butter on poached or grilled fish, deep-fried parsley sprigs with fried fish.

* Fry bread shapes in olive oil and butter to make large croûtons for garnishing casseroles and sauced dishes. Crescent shapes look good.

* Shred filo pastry, brush lightly with melted butter and bake until crisp. Serve as a garnish for sauced and steamed dishes.

* Shred green cabbage, deep-fry for a few seconds and toss in a little caster sugar. Serve as a garnish for Chinese-style stir-fries.

* Shred an omelette into strips or cut out shapes and use to garnish rice or noodle dishes, or serve in clear soups, such as chicken bouillon.

* Shred or cut out pancake shapes to garnish soups.

* Boil quails' eggs for 3 minutes, drain, shell and cut them in half for garnishing pâtés, starters, open sandwiches and salads.

Steamed salmon with herbs.

Boiled quails' eggs make an unusual garnish for salad and pasta dishes.

Salmon salad with star-shaped croûtons.

SWEET DECORATIONS

WHIPPING CREAM

✹ Whipped cream is still one of the most popular decorations for topping desserts, piping over gâteaux or finishing fresh fruit. It is easy to spoil the look of a dessert, however, by overwhipping the cream and ending up with a buttery, slightly yellow appearance.

✹ Double cream whips well to give a good piping consistency and will hold its shape when piped.

✹ Whipping cream has a lower fat content than double. It whips to a softer consistency, but with greater volume; however, it will not hold its shape as well when piped and can sag slightly on standing. Whipping cream is ideal for loosely swirling in generous proportions on individual desserts.

TIPS FOR CREAM

✹ A good alternative to whipping cream is to add 30ml/2 tbsp milk to 300ml/½ pint/1¼ cups double cream as this lightens the cream and gives a good volume as well as structure.

✹ Chill all utensils before whipping cream. Whip it until it holds its shape in soft peaks, then stop. If double cream is whipped beyond this point, it will stiffen and, eventually, separate, becoming buttery and fatty in texture.

✹ For Chantilly cream, add a little natural vanilla essence and icing sugar to whipping cream. Whip the cream just before serving it, then spoon it over desserts.

Cream complements most desserts.

POURING-CREAM DECORATIONS

✹ These are added at the last minute, just before the dessert is presented at the table.

✹ Drop dots of single cream into dark sauces, such as chocolate, coffee or raspberry purée, then drag a cocktail stick through the middle of the cream to feather it into the sauce.

✹ Trickle short lines of single cream into fruit purées or dark sauces, or into deeply coloured fruit fools, then swirl the cream lightly with the point of a knife or a skewer. Take care not to make too many swirls or the effect will be lost.

FROSTED LEAVES AND FLOWERS

Right: Brush rose petals or mint or lemon balm leaves in a little lightly whisked egg white.

Above: Sprinkle generously with caster sugar.
Right: Leave on non-stick baking paper until dry and crisp.

CHOCOLATE-DIPPED FRUIT

Fresh strawberries, grapes, cherries, physalis, mandarin or clementine segments can all be dipped in melted chocolate. Melt dark or white chocolate in a small heatproof bowl over a saucepan of hot, not

Chocolate-dipped fruit.

simmering, water. Have a sheet of non-stick baking paper ready on a baking sheet. Wash and dry the fruit, folding back the papery, lantern-shaped covering on physalis and leaving stalks on. Dip half the fruit in melted chocolate, allow the excess to drip off, then place it on the paper to set.

TIPS FOR FINISHING TOUCHES

✳ Crushed biscuits, such as ratafias or brandy snaps, make a contrasting topping for soft desserts such as set creams.

✳ Sift icing sugar lightly over fresh fruit just before taking it to the table.

✳ Finely grated chocolate can be sprinkled over creamy desserts and cakes.

✳ Cocoa can be sifted lightly over chocolate desserts.

✳ Serve desserts on large plates with a fashionable dusting of icing sugar to enhance the appearance of dark china.

✳ Frost rose petals or violets (see facing page) and use to decorate desserts or the plates on which they are presented.

CANDIED PEEL RIBBONS

Make this in the latter part of winter when the new season's citrus fruit is available. To preserve the individual flavour of each fruit – lemons, limes and oranges – they should all be candied separately.

Citrus fruit can be candied whole or in slices.

Makes approximately 675g/1½ lb

INGREDIENTS
5 large oranges or 10 lemons or limes, unwaxed
675g/1½ lb granulated sugar, plus extra for
sprinkling

Cut the fruit in half, squeeze out the juice and discard the flesh, but not the pith.

Cut the peel into strips about 1cm/½ in wide and place in a pan, cover with boiling water and simmer for five minutes.

Drain, then repeat four times, using fresh water each time to remove the peel's natural bitterness.

In a heavy-based saucepan, pour 250ml/8fl oz/ 1 cup water over the sugar; heat, stirring, to dissolve the sugar. Add the peel, cover partially and cook slowly for 30–40 minutes, until soft.

Leave to cool thoroughly, then sprinkle with sugar.

PASTRY TRIMMINGS

CUT-OUT EDGE

Use cocktail or aspic cutters to stamp out shapes from rolled-out pastry. Brush the edge of the pie, tart or flan with a little water and overlap the pastry shapes on the pastry base.

Cut-out edge.

RIBBON EDGE

Cut out long, even strips, measuring 2cm/¾ in wide, from rolled-out pastry. Dampen the edge of the pastry and press the end of one strip on to it. Twist the strip gently and press it on the edge again. Continue all the way around the edge.

Ribbon edge.

PASTRY LATTICE

Roll out the pastry on a lightly floured surface. Cut out a circle that is a little larger than the pie dish. Then cut the round into neat, even strips, using a ruler and a knife or fluted pastry wheel.

Lay half the pastry strips across the top of the filling, taking care to keep them parallel and evenly spaced. Leave the excess of each strip overhanging the edge of the dish.

Fold back every other strip from the centre. Lay another strip across the centre, on the flat strips and at right angles to them. Lay the folded strips flat. Fold back the strips that were not folded the first time. Lay a strip of pastry across the flat ones, spacing it evenly from the central one. Replace the folded strips. Continue folding the strips on this side and on the other half of the pie. Trim the edges of the strips, dampen the pastry rim, lifting each of the strips as you do so, then press them in place.

A lattice crust looks very effective.

SHORTCRUST PASTRY

Makes one 23cm/9in pastry case

INGREDIENTS
225g/8oz/2 cups plain flour
1.5ml/¼ tsp salt
115g/4oz/½ cup margarine, chilled and diced
45–60ml/3–4 tbsp iced water

Combine the flour, salt and diced margarine in the bowl of a food processor. Process, turning the machine on and off, just until the mixture is crumbly. Add the iced water and process again briefly – until the dough starts to pull away from the sides of the bowl. Remove the dough from the processor and gather it into a ball. Wrap and refrigerate.

Wrap the dough in clear film and refrigerate.

FRENCH FLAN PASTRY

Makes one 23cm/9in pastry case

INGREDIENTS
200g/7oz/1¾ cups plain flour
2.5 ml/½ tsp salt
115g/4oz/½ cup butter or margarine, chilled
1 egg yolk
1.5ml/¼ tsp lemon juice
30–45ml/2–3tbsp iced water

Sift the flour and salt into a bowl. Rub the butter into the flour until the mixture begins to clump together.

In a small bowl, mix egg yolk, lemon juice and 2 tbsp water. Add to the flour mixture. With a fork, toss gently to mix and moisten. Press the dough into a rough ball and tip onto a work surface. With the heel of your hand, push small portions of dough away from you, smearing them on the surface. Continue mixing the dough until it feels pliable but not sticky. Press the dough into a ball. Wrap in clear film and chill for at least 30 minutes.

TIPS FOR PASTRY-MAKING

* Reflour the surface and rolling pin if the dough starts to stick.
* If the dough tears, patch with a piece of moistened dough.
* Once or twice during rolling out, gently push in the edges of the dough with your cupped palms, to keep the circular shape.
* A pastry scraper will help lift the dough from the work surface to wrap it around the rolling pin.

INDEX